Thomas Beddoes

Alternatives compared,

Or, What shall the rich do to be safe?

Thomas Beddoes

Alternatives compared,
Or, What shall the rich do to be safe?

ISBN/EAN: 9783337732677

Printed in Europe, USA, Canada, Australia, Japan

Cover: Foto ©ninafisch / pixelio.de

More available books at **www.hansebooks.com**

ALTERNATIVES

COMPARED:

OR,

WHAT SHALL THE RICH DO

TO

BE SAFE?

Tremo che tu non fcelga infra i partiti
Per più certo il più dannofo——

By THOMAS BEDDOES, M. D.

London:

PRINTED FOR J. DEBRETT, OPPOSITE BURLINGTON HOUSE,
PICCADILLY.
M.DCC.XCVII.

WHAT SHALL THE RICH DO

BE SAFE?

~~~~~~

I HAVE heard it remarked, by a fhrewd and fuccefsful trader, that *a man is faved in the next world by faith*; *in this, by the want of it.* In whom you fhall confide is feldom a point of flight deliberation; and, in many emergencies, you perifh or efcape, according as you decide. The frowning afpect of the prefent juncture fummons the great to enter into ferious and fincere council with themfelves. The paft muft be revifed, that provifion may be made for the future. The evidence of the crifis is ftrong and full. The parties concerned are required but to approach it with docility, and to fit upon their own fate, as true and uncorrupt jurors, divefted of all prejudgments. They muft not forget that there is a difpofition indifpenfable to the difcovery of political

B   cal

cal as well as phyfical truth. Let them be content to take themfelves only for what they are; fubjects and interpreters, not arbitrary comptrollers, of the laws of nature. This doctrine of philofophical humility may not be very congenial to the temper of thofe accuftomed to be obeyed. Without it, however, all examination of men and things will be fruitlefs. And it would be perhaps lefs wafte of time to ftudy the prodigies of the Apocalypfe; that, by contemplating the calamities of imagination, they may learn to fuftain thofe of reality with greater fortitude.

" How are the poffeffors of influence to exert it for their own and the public fecurity ? Shall they continue, recklefs and paffive, in their leading-ftrings ? adopt a temporifing fyftem ? or endeavour, in union with their inferiors, to obtain a change of men and meafures ?" Thefe queftions the hurricane of events has to-day brought full before them : yet a little while, and they will be fwept out of their competence for ever.

That defperate attachment of the Great, which has emboldened a rafh adminiftration to embark in fo many defperate fchemes, is not wholly to be afcribed to favouritifm. This weaknefs never affects many individuals in the fame manner. The paradoxical public conduct which we have fo long witneffed in our wealthy countrymen is not to be

ex-

explained by saying that they have found, for succeffive years, a perverfe pleafure in humouring the caprices of a junto. To enable one member to chuck rupees by lacks into the pockets of his India dependents, and another to indulge a childifh vanity in fhewing the world what fine things he can do for his family and friends, is not a purpofe capable of uniting fo numerous a body.

I am likewife far from imputing to the Britifh nobility that felfifhnefs, which, if we may believe Doctor Smith, proved fatal to the confequence of their precurfors, the ancient barons. They do not take for their motto, *all for ourfelves, and nothing for other people* (Wealth of Nations, ii. 125); but they doubtlefs feel well inclined to keep to themfelves what they have to themfelves. Idlenefs and vanity are not purely Patrician qualities. We of Plebeian origin have wherewithal to appreciate the convenience of being honourable, independently of merit: and he who has learned but as much of the effects of pride, habit, and poffefflon, as every man may learn without going out of himfelf, will fcarce expect the proprietors of privilege to confent that all infants fhould be ftarted into life upon the fame footing of privilege. Does any one defcry Innovation about to rob his offspring, with intent to fet up their birth-right as a prize, for which the vulgar are to have the right of entering the lifts ? That parent will be judged to betray a difgraceful

want

want of natural feeling, if he ftop long to calcu-
late rifks, before he refolves to oppofe himfelf to
the injuftice.

The landed commoner or country gentleman I
confider as endowed with no lefs acutenefs of fenfibility towards conventional refpectability than his
fuperior in precedence. Looking forward to rank,
and morally affimilated to the peer, he will, in
cafes of danger to hereditary diftinctions, be
equally actuated by felf-love, parental love, love
of eafe, of enjoyment, and pre-eminence. They
will both agree to make the caufe of their fellows
in another country their own.

Thefe fears, and this fympathy, drew his ancient adherents clofer round the minifter, and
brought new crowds of followers to his ftandard.
All were eager to quell the example of civic equa-
lity in France. In the fenfe of the Britifh no-
bleffe, the conteft had no other object; nor, without this end in view, fhould we ever have engaged
in it.

I appeal to the paft language and prefent perfuafion of the affluent and the noble. It was not
in a fquabble about the choice of regicides in
which they meant to take part. That a baffled in-
triguer, intent folely upon bilking difgrace, fhould
affert the capacity of *this* in preference to *that*

horde

horde of levellers to maintain the relations of peace and amity, is an occurrence to which parallels may be found in all the records of ambitious hypocrify. But Lord Fitzwilliam's numerous affociates in political fentiment, whenever they hear expofitions of the object of the war foftened down to exifting circumftances, muft fmile contempt upon the fubterfuge. Each confcious countenance muft declare to the other—

Non hæc in fœdera veni.

What the minifter wifhes is plain enough. He would have the encouragement given by himfelf, and by his partners in power, to the ftrong defire and fanguine hope of re-eftablifhing whatever had been overturned in France blotted from memory. No wonder——He has his fufficient reafons. He may dread left their baulked expectations fhould warn his fupporters againft trufting for *fecurity* to that front and thofe tones which fo lately promifed *conqueft*. It can certainly afford him little fatisfaction to have the Mr. Pitt of 1793 compared with that Mr. Pitt, who, in 1796, ftooped to receive, among the full-coiffed and long-robed governments of Europe, a bald, unkinged, unpriefted democracy, fhorn of ever-green honours, and gay with no budding diftinctions. He muft be aware, that Mr. Pitt's whole confequence with foreign nations and future ages depended upon fuccefs in dragooning the French into fubmiffion.

Four

Four years ago, many a folitary half hour may have glided imperceptibly away, while he was bufy in thinking whofe image would offer itfelf to the fpectators of the victorious march of the confederates into Paris; heading the legions, eclipfing the generals, auguft beyond mortality, and every moment borrowing increafe of majefty from the rekindling luftre of a father's triumphs. Then, belike, *" his great mind,"* buoyant upon a balloon of vifions, *" was up to the crifis he is called to act in."* Ere this, the babler has probably fubfided to humbler ideas of his deftiny; and he may be fenfible that a mock-ftatue, exhibiting him among the founders of the new republic, would be the emblem moft fuitable to the eftimation in which he is doomed to be held.

· The inability of adminiftration to crufh the monfter JACOBINISM having been acknowledged by their own moft public acts, what courfe remains for the champions of the old temporal and fpiritual authorities in France? Are they to rufh on in blindfold confiftency? Or has the caufe of focial order fo irretrievably fuffered in the hands of a heaven-born ftatefman, that to mention further efforts in its behalf founds like infulting the unhappy with their misfortunes?

One ardent mind has been proof againft defpair, as maniacs refift the benumbing power of

an

An arctic winter. I speak of that singular statesman, whose phrenzy has of late been regarded as prophetic, though it had used to pass for the mere symptom of vulgar mental disorder. The found majority of the Britons are advised by this, their oracle, to tend at all hazards for the same point, striking however into a new road, but following the old guides, as if, after all, their fidelity and intelligence were nothing to be questioned.

From the constancy with which the nation sustained the difficulties of an eighteen years against Louis XIV. our undaunted veteran infers the reasonableness of perseverance. We know what was the noble incentive of our forefathers: nor will I waste a moment in inquiring whether the people can be instigated by the zeal of liberty to second the views of the present ministry at the hazard of life and fortune. I will only try how the precedent applies in another way. A magnanimous monarch, we are told, formed a vast design " *on true mechanical principles.*" His workmanship did not disgrace his conceptions. The machine, as long as its powers were needed, went on by the impulse it received from its inventor's hand. So much for WILLIAM, the monarch. Next comes WILLIAM, the minister. Under his superintendance, the machinery of the state seems clogged, and ready to run into disorder. The public concerns have little of the exte-

rior

rior of profperity. Hence we feel difcouraged; but we are perhaps difcouraged by deceitful appearances. Clofe fearch may difclofe grounds for expecting final fuccefs. There are undertakings, and thofe not the leaft lucrative, where the returns at the outfet are fmall, becaufe the judicious application of labour and capital has enfured ample future compenfation. Our advocate for confidence is doubtlefs prepared to fhew, that our ftate-engineer has completed his works in a mafterly manner, and that only a little further advance is wanting to put them in motion.

This is the only method of arguing which his fide of the queftion admits; by no other, if they have only a legal lot of difcretion, can thofe who have to find means be made to reft fatisfied with him who undertakes to find method. Let us fee how the point is handled :

" *Through the falfe policy of the war, the greateft fkill has been worfe than ufelefsly employed to conduct the greateft military apparatus. The whole has been but one error. The war ought not to have been a war of calculation. It was matter of choice; yet the enemy was attacked where he was invincible; fpared where he was ready to diffolve by his own internal diforders. Our plan was neither good for offence nor defence. They (we) adopted a plan of war, againft the fuccefs of which there was fomething little fhort of mathematical demonftration. They (we) acted*
through

*through the whole, as if really wishing the conservation
of the Jacobin power."*

Such is our British directory in council. Their
magnanimity and wisdom have entitled them to
equal applause in debate. The present miniftry,
says Mr. Burke, " *throw the light only on one side
of their cause. They never entered into the peculiar
and diftinctive character of the war. They spoke
neither to the underftanding, nor the heart. Cold as
ice themfelves, they could never kindle in our breafts
a spark of that zeal which is neceffary to a conflict
with an adverfe zeal.*" The found majority of the
nation have " *never fo much as had the queftion
fairly ftated to them.*"

Such is the logic of the ableft and beft paid
advocate of adminiftration. And there is the
lefs to be apprehended from his rhetoric, fince he
has this time fo compounded his *protreptic*, as to
deftroy its intoxicating effect. By fo difcoidant a
tune no liftener can be fimple enough to be piped
into a perfuafion that, under this adminiftration,
" *what has been loft in the field, in the field may be
regained.*" Dramatic writers, after exhibiting a
rake, wild and thoughtlefs, through more than
four acts, fometimes difmifs us with his fudden
transformation into the decent, ftaid mafter of a
family. And fo much has been allowed to poetic
licenfe. But there exifts a fenfelefs prodigality,

C   which

which it is not poffible to conceive corrected into thrifty wifdom. The inftant converfion of Mr. Pitt and his accomplices into a cabinet capable of refcuing us from the ftate to which blood and treafures lavifhed "*for fupport of the Jacobin fyftem*" have reduced us, ftands confpicuous among the examples of prodigy that defy imagination.

Exhortation, therefore, is vain. The great will concur no more in a fyftem of hoftilities directed to the overthrow of republicanifm. The frantic paroxyfm is paft. But who can tell by what fatal torpor it is to be fucceeded? They who refufe the precipice, by allowing themfelves to flide down the flope, may equally get into the gulf which lies at the bottom of both. There is a fyftem lefs outrageous, but not lefs ruinous than exterminating war; and into this I fear left the favourites of fortune fhould be betrayed by the joint operation of habit, attachment, and example. Thofe who know any thing of the higher orders in fociety, know their general impatience of continued attention. Have they ferious bufinefs? It muft be brought before them prepared for inftant difpatch :—it would be too troublefome to difentangle its perplexities. They cannot be put out of their lazy, pick-tooth mood. So their agent always fees a fine fertile field of fraud open before him. To thefe fame votaries of indolence the minifter is only a fteward, with more repulfive reckon-
ings.

ings. Him, therefore, they audit with lefs awaken-
ed ear, and he finds his facility of impofition as
much greater as his concerns are larger than thofe
of the private fteward.

Again, fufferings we have neither experienced
nor feen excite in us but a lukewarm fympathy.
The mourning of decency refolves itfelf into a
procefs of the art of dying : the pity of decency is an
affair of words. Twenty thoufand poor families
ftarved, an unknown and countlefs rabble killed
off, without interruption to their enjoyments, will
have no fyftematic influence on the conduct of the
mafs of the affluent, however well they may be
difpofed. Except in individuals of reflection more
than commonly exercifed, the fmalleft oppofite
paffion will be more than a counterbalance for
commiferation. To the reft, the idea of the execu-
tion of a minifter will be a thoufand times more
fhocking than all this mifery, and all this carnage.

The cafe of a former war minifter is in the memory of many, in the knowledge of us all. It
will be allowed, that there ought to be terrors to
keep back folly, as well as villainy, from the helm
of affairs. Regard to human fafety does not eafily
run into over-delicacy. When a domeftic animal is
by chance the death of any member of a family, he
is, very properly, put for ever out of fight, though
moral turpitude be not imputable to the brute crea-

tion.

tion. After the American war, how did this protective feeling operate as to Lord North? I know not whether he was from the firſt averſe to that difaſtrous enterprize; but, when it had become deſperate, he perſiſted in it with an obſtinacy againſt which there ought ſurely to be ſome ſafeguard for men's lives as much as againſt malice aforethought. The moſt guilty motives were aſſigned to his conduct. Mr. Burke, I think, charged the miniſtry with perſevering to ſhed blood, merely becauſe they could not make peace and continue a miniſtry. Lord North, notwithſtanding, was brought to no account; no brand was ſet upon him; the name of a private criminal excited more horror; nay, he carried with him out of office every thing but miniſterial influence. He went into retirement, not into diſgrace; he ſtill held his head high in the ſenate; and, what in an ancient hiſtorian would appear incredible, after all the havoc in which he had borne ſo principal a ſhare, he enjoyed, perhaps, more conſideration than any Britiſh ſtateſman. How great was his conſequence in Mr. Fox's judgment, while the gaſhes he had inflicted on his country were ſtill uncloſed, appeared from the famous coalition.

From Lord North's example I conclude that the great, in ſpite of ſome interruption to their enjoyments from the prevailing alarms, will, in general, feel no active or laſting indignation againſt

Mr,

Mr. Pitt. However they may diftruft or condemn the minifter, they will ftill fcreen the man. He will defire time either to frame new pretexts for continuing in office, or to compofe his fkirts as he retreats. In either cafe, whatever be the danger of temporifing, he will have no caufe to complain of want of complaifance on the part of his old fupporters.

On a fuperficial review of our hiftory, it may be vainly fuppofed, that peace and war are for ever to fucceed each other like the feafons: the fummer of peace, as if by a natural neceffity, regularly repairing the ravages of war. Treachery lurks even under the example of the American war. The iffue with regard to America failed to make us paufe over the difficulty of forcing laws upon an unwilling people. The iffue with regard to ourfelves, may render us too little fenfible to the danger of having once more engaged in a fimilar adventure. A familiar fpirit is faid to have admonifhed Socrates from wrong. Some people have internal feelings, by which they can judge with how much of active and paffive fortitude the determination to be free can infpire others. The heart of Mr. Pitt does not appear to have been *lefs* fufceptible of thefe feelings than that of Lord North; nor in his fucceffive military meafures has he been *more* unfortunate or unwife. But what a difference in the abfolute and relative circumftances cumſtances of the two nations, againſt which theſe two politicians have had to contend! We cannot imagine the tranſatlantic conſtitution to partake ſo much of aſbeſtos, that no provocation could inflame the love of liberty into ambition and vengeance. But as the two parties viewed the deſigns of the Britiſh cabinet, the Americans would feel rather leſs enraged. For to tax unrepreſented colonies is ſomewhat a leſs violent proceeding than to conquer and divide a great independent ſtate. This laſt is the greateſt of political injuries, aggravated by the greateſt of inſults. The French may have been falſely, but they ſeem to have been generally perſuaded, that a worſe than Poliſh outrage was deſigned them. What has been done to draw this ſting that rankles in their minds? We entered no proteſt againſt the *eagle of Valenciennes.* Even the treaty of Pilnitz has not been publiſhed by authority; yet its publication, if it contain no article of this flagrant tendency, would go far towards generating amicable ſentiments.

America, whatever might have been her inclination, was not in a ſtate to paſs from defence to offence; ſhe had no means of putting in force the barbarous law of retaliation; we had but to withdraw, and the conteſt was at an end; there were hardly two parties to a pacification. The other contending powers deſired but the diſunion of the daughter from the parent ſtate. With the French, war

war was far from having loft that character under which it exhibited itfelf a century ago, when it was a fummer fport for the *grand monarque*.

There are, I think, four alternatives between which our prefent fituation permits us the choice :

1. We may call back the miniftry, as it is at this moment conftituted, to the original purpofe of hoftilities, which was nothing lefs than the *unconditional fubmiffion* of the republicans.

2. We may exert ourfelves to promote the fubftitution of difciples of the fchool of Burke, in the room of the prefent Chancellor of the Exchequer and certain of his colleagues. Thofe who have been rendered

" —— fiercer by defpair "

have no excufe, but in the infirmities of declining years, for forbearing to call the MASTER himfelf into a fituation to help to make good what he propofes.

3. We may acquiefce in the part to which we are reduced when we defire a change of the wind. We may fit quiet, wifhing that *things would come round.*

Upon

Upon the eligibility of either of thefe three meafures it would be wafte of words to fay more. It remains to ftate and examine the fourth.

4. We may beftir ourfelves againft the miniftry with as much alertnefs as if we had to refcue all we hold dear from a building in flames.

I know not how it fares with others, who, when *the rulers took council together and the multitude were* TAUGHT *to imagine a vain thing*, forefaw and foretold the difafters that were preparing. For myfelf, I can neither feel nor exprefs myfelf with equal warmth. Is it that fome minds are touched to the quick by enormities detected in the meditation? Is indignation a feeling which cannot maintain itfelf long in its original force? Or is it blunted by contempt for the authors of evil, when their machinations have been blafted? Every juft prognoftic muft be followed by more or lefs of felf-approbation. Can felf-approbation foften us towards the betrayers and deftroyers of mankind? — He that fimply defired to fave the unwary may have yet a more cogent reafon for ftating calmly the evils of which he had forewarned with vehemence. He may know that the contrary exercife of rhetoric is often but the triumph of malignity over diftrefs; and he can never fuppofe words capable of conveying

fo

fo exact an idea of phenomena as the fenfes themfelves.

The public condition is, in moft cafes, a fuffi-cient teft of the ability of thofe who have long managed the public concerns. To compare Great Britain as it is, with Great Britain as it was, requires no labour of refearch. The diftinguifhing cir-cumftances are obvious to fight : and they are within a narrow field of vifion. We *had* a com-merce fuch as human induftry had never before created ; we *had* unbounded credit ; a revenue in-creafing ; a public debt decreafing, and capable (under wifer management) of a rapid reduction ; fpecie was driven in to us from all parts of Europe. The repute of the paper of the Bank of England was not only untarnifhed by fufpicion, but its notes were often preferred to cafh. We had attained that *prof-perity* which, to politicians by profeffion, is the fu-preme good ; and which the political philofopher may regret, when it is redeemed by no diffufed and popular bleffings. In a rapid decline of five years, our great ftaple manufactories have been reduced almoft to fufpenfion ; the merchant is faddened by the blank profpect of full and undifturbed ware-houfes ; the new orders are infufficient for that half-ftarved remnant of workmen, whom unwhole-fome climates and the fword have not yet de-ftroyed. The languid movement of commerce is principally forced by the pernicious ftimulus of

D war ;

war; fpecie is difappearing; credit expiring; the
circulating capital dwindling; the fixed capital
threatened with dilapidation; the apprehenfion of
that laft of all evils to a commercial people, a
forced paper currency, gaining ground; the pro-
longation of the war next to impoffible; peace
difficult to obtain; and, at this critical moment, our
neareft and moft remote dependencies are in a ftate
of progreffive difcontent, threatening civil diftur-
bances. The wifh for an afylum has croffed the mind
of many a father, anxious for his family; and corps
of volunteers are forming at home, avowedly, among
other purpofes, to protect property and perfons
againft plunder and outrage. That precious in-
heritance which every Englifhman derived from
the exalted reputation of his country, is irretrievably gone. We fhall rank no more as

" —— lords of human kind."

Nice obfervers of the emotions muft often have
noticed in the firft indeliberate animation of the
moft loyal emigrant, on the report of republican
fucceffes, a fure indication of their effect on national characters. Henceforward, whenever they
meet in a country foreign to both, the Frenchman,
inftead of giving way as formerly, will think himfelf entitled to elbow our countryman.

We

We have here no short catalogue of calamities; and they come too near to thofe, in whofe defcription, when they afflicted France, the minifter and his favourers loved to riot. Added to this, we have an adverfary lynx-eyed to difcern, and fwift to feize her advantages: an adverfary that has juft converted her forced paper into fpecie, her enemies into allies, her anarchy into order. We have a miniftry with whom nothing has been more familiar than declarations of fatisfaction, all the time the affairs of the two countries have been in full ftraight forward fpeed to the points they have refpectively attained.

Thefe grofs facts will fatisfy every fincere inquirer. It is fcarce neceffary he fhould be told how often the conductors of our affairs have rejected the invitations of opportunity to maintain or to reftore peace. What happened fifteen years ago muft immediately happen again. The people will become univerfally perfuaded, *that the prefent men are not the men either for a peace fyftem or a war fyftem.* To this perfuafion will fucceed juft aftonifhment, how individuals, poffeffing certain talents with means of information, could conceive the ideas on which the authors of this train of misfortunes have proceeded; and how millions of rational beings could tamely behold their deareft interefts entrufted to perfons capable of fuch wild conceptions, and enterprizes fo infane.

The

The principal departments of ſtate are filled by perſons of three deſcriptions. Among the laſt appointed, one man only ſtands forward with pretenſions. Mr. —— is diſtinguiſhed chiefly by intemperance of mind. His language, when his aſſociates are not obliged to condemn him to ſilence, breathes the genuine ſpirit of cannibaliſm; and it is difficult not to ſuppoſe that he could feaſt with pleaſure upon the heart of one whom he ſhould be pleaſed to ſtile a Jacobin, provided the culprit belonged to the number of his ancient friends. His paſſions, ungovernable as they may ſeem, do yet in reality ebb and flow at another's nod. Notwithſtanding his furious and indiſcriminate invectives, it is ſcarce a matter of doubtful hiſtory that he was an approving ſpectator of the early ſcenes of the revolution in France. We are certain that he is the author of no meaſure that might not have been conceived by the moſt ordinary perſon, waking or aſleep. Charity will diſmiſs him with a wiſh that his laſt moments may not be haunted by the ſpectre of the gallant ——, eſcorted by a train of butchered emigrants.

Upon the whole ſecond diviſion, hiſtory had pronounced. Their names were committed to everlaſting memory; for they figured among the projectors and conductors of the war againſt our American colonies. Was it from diſſatisfaction with the diſtinction they had already obtained that they

they gave once more the reins to ambition? Without doubt, their avarice of fame muft at length be fatiated. They have been favoured beyond the lot of their fellows. The varied annals of mankind furnifh no inftance where a knot of politicians have been permitted by fate to advance fo far in a fecond career, after completing, as *they* completed, the firft.

The people feem never to have repofed in thefe fages the confidence which talents, joined to experience, commonly command. It was as if they enjoyed power by public connivance rather than public deference. If it be true that the moft fecret thoughts are drawn forth by the power of wine, it muft be moft true of thofe who have been leaft practifed to diffemble. Yet in 1793, when the multitude, intoxicated with liquor and with lies, difturbed all the echoes of the kingdom with cries for war, did any one hear the names of Jenkinfon or Wedderburne, of Eden or Dundas, pronounced with applaufe or expectation?

All hopes refted upon a man, comparatively raw in every concern of ftate, and abfolutely a novice in the conduct of war. On Mr. Pitt confidence was originally beftowed; and to him, as far as the miniftry at prefent enjoy confidence, they owe its continuance: he, therefore, becomes the great object of attention in the prefent ftage of our inquiry. Should it appear that the origin of his extensive popularity was *extraneous* or independent of merit and fervices, and that his faculties of heart and head are in unifon with the diftreffes of the ftate, it would be no longer problematical to whom we are to lay the difafters we endure, and the dangers we dread.

Divines have been at pains to delineate the fituation of the human race on the appearance of the Meffiah.—The ftate of Britain, towards the clofe of the American war, requires no elaborate defcription. The deluded, injured, and almoft defpairing, inhabitants had long been panting for a deliverer. What is there ftrange, when a people, thus difpofed, are tranfported beyond prudence by the firft ray of hope? Lefs than a defcendant and a namefake of their idol, Chatham, with the fhadow of his father's talents, would, at fuch a moment, foothe their fufferings, and difpel their apprehenfions. If they yielded to firft fpecious appearances, they only committed an act of precipitancy, againft which neither the leffons of hiftory nor the actual experience of calamity have been fufficient to warn the mafs of mankind. The abufe of credulity, arifing in part from goodnefs of heart, ferves but to deepen the guilt of ambition ; as we abhor an affaffin the more for murdering the traveller, who, at a dangerous pafs, too eafily accepts his proffered protection.

The

The nature of language fhould render us fearful, left we deceive ourfelves or others when we employ general terms. There are few terms more fallacious than *ability*, when it is ufed alone. In, many cafes, the poffeffor of certain endowments or acquirements is afferted or denied to be *able*; and the difpute becomes interminable, lefs for want of facts than for want of a previous fettlement of the precife import which the word is to bear on the occafion. This ambiguity is the perpetual plague of political difputants.

Some powers of mind and body are far from implying other powers. There are even powers from which you may with confidence infer, that the poffeffor is deficient in certain other powers. There is no reafon to fuppofe, becaufe a paffenger on board is an *able* dancer on the flack rope, that he is fit to take the helm when the fhip is in diftrefs. The chances are much againft your fcullion being clever at her needle; her occupation will make her hands too clumfy.

Mr. Pitt, beyond queftion, poffeffes *abilities*. His fuperior excellence, at leaft one of his great excellencies, confifts in a good arrangement of words, and accompanied by a good utterrance. The laft qualifies, to a certain degree, for the ftage; in no refpect for the council-board. It will not be contended, that there exifts a law of nature, which

conftitutes

conftitutes the rival of Mrs. Siddons the fuperior of Sully.

The voluble recitation of *your own* thoughts is but a femi-theatrical talent. The art, though unknown as a feparate art in this age, flourifhed in Greece; and the more its profeffors, the SOPHISTS, came to be known, the lefs were they and their art efteemed. If it be defirable to eftimate rightly the character of a man who has played fuch a part among his countrymen as Mr. Pitt, this hiftorical fact is of great importance.

Were the difficult art of walking of no more general ufe than finging, it would not be more common. It is not neceffary to the maintenance of many people that they fhould carry on the two proceffes of fpeaking and thinking, with uniform celerity, long together. But almoft all men, except ideots and incurable ftammerers, may be taught this knack; as certainly, not, perhaps, fo fpeedily, as to move harmonically to founds, or to work a hand-faw and whiftle. To touch with dexterity two rows of notes on the harpfichord would, in all probability, be found to require more application. A difference, without doubt, would appear in the attainments of different fcholars; but not fuch as to deferve to be confidered in delegating an important national truft.

Your

Your pupil, if he have no glaring external or internal blemifh, may not only be expected to become a proficient in declamation, but, as a collateral benefit of his education, he will probably acquire propenfities of no mean effect in civil intercourfe. He will come forth among mankind, oftentatious, fubtle, overbearing, and felfifh ; or, at leaft, fully prepared to make any progrefs in thefe difpofitions. In all refpects he muft be the oppofite—I do not fay of the philofopher, for the title is become opprobrious—but of him who, in fincerity, feeks the truth, and communicates what he believes.

It is his care *how* to fpeak, not *what* to think. In qualifying himfelf to harangue for any length of time upon either fide of any queftion, he is labouring precifely to become double-tongued. He will have profited little by the difcipline to which he has fubmitted, if it have not rendered him dexterous in enfnaring the incautious. This familiarity with fraud is of itfelf dangerous ; and every thing here confpires to favour its debafing operation. By perpetual endeavours to infufe opinions into others, he eftablifhes the habit of referring all their feelings to himfelf. To him, therefore, mankind will be eftimable, odious, or indifferent, according to the attention they fhall pay the object towards which he takes fo much pains to draw their regard. Nor can we fuppofe that he will feel

E   difinclined

difinclined to meafures which may force the appearance, when he finds he cannot win the reality.
It is not an indifferent circumftance that every
difplay of oratory muft be perfonal. He who can
exhibit his powers, without the neceffity of wit-
neffing the effect, incurs, in a much lefs degree,
the hazard of a corrupt mind. For human frailty
will fubmit to unremitting temptation; and, at
length, no artifices will be left uneffayed by the
performer to furprize the judgment of his audience.
Then Vanity receives the fubmiffions of her flave.
Then fhe burns her mark into his mind; and, for
a daily tafk, affigns him the fabrication of gins and
traps to catch the applaufe of fools.

To this reafoning, the example of the modern
advocate will be oppofed. But the ftudies of the
modern advocate are as little calculated to form
him to the refemblance of the ancient fophift as
to render him a difinterefted lover of truth and juftice. Nothing forbade the fophift to linger on the
fmooth and flowery lawn of a common topic.
And he could range the wilds of paradox at will.
But in our courts and caufes there are checks upon
the wanton excurfions of eloquence. In the
fchools of fophiftry there was nothing on which
you could faften. All was fhadowy and fictitious.
But in atteftations, precedents, and ftatutes, there
is fomething folid, by which to fix the underftanding, and to hold it to moorings.

Rhetorical

Rhetorical trimmings appear ill to fuit the mind that is dreffed in the fad and folemn garb of law. Our lawyers are not often poets, or fine writers; their ftudies do not feem exceedingly compatible with a tafte for the elegancies of literature; nor, in fact, when they fpeak, are they found much to excel ordinary men in the talent of trundling the round and polifhed period* over the tongue.

Mr. Pitt's accomplifhments and defects unite to declare how much the dangerous art of declamation muft have been the object of his early affiduity. His lips feem never touched by the hallowed fire of genius. No fentiment ftrikes you as if projected by natural energy of mind. I know not how many weeks or months the hours he has harangued, added together, would make. But if, with fuch abundant opportunities, he be the only celebrated fpeaker, from whom have iffued none of thofe brilliant or profound fallies which nations delight to repeat, the fact will fhew how much the *mechanical* predominates over the *mental* ingredient in his orations.

You go along with him to the midft of an intricate period. You tremble for his grammar; but your apprehenfions are premature. The moft ex-

* Mellitos verborum globulos.

pert

pert artifan has not a hand furer than his tongue.
This aptnefs can be no other than the refult of
continually reiterated efforts. His father, perhaps,
knew not how to elevate and enlarge his conceptions; but he was able, and it is not to be doubted
but he was earneft, to beftow on the fon whom he
deftined to figure in debate, that part of eloquence
which confifts in affortment of words, in well-,
fafhioned phrafes, and in tones.

By an acquaintance and a clofe obferver of the
late Lord Chatham I have heard it faid, that he
himfelf fubmitted to read the Englifh dictionary
fix times over. I think it was after he had acquired fome diftinction in the Houfe of Commons.
It is not neceffary for me to make an application
of the anecdote.

To folid men of bufinefs all this care of founds
would appear frivolous. They know that whatever is worth faying can be comprehended in few
and unculled words. The obfervation of mankind has not only taught them, that a fupple
tongue has no neceffary connection with effective
talents; but that it ought to render a man fufpected, as well with regard to his integrity as his
efficiency. Oilinefs of articulation, accompanied
with a diction of ftudied foftnefs, they reckon
among the fureft figns of an incapable impoftor.
It is a fyren fong, which men are feldom found to
learn,

learn, but that they may overreach others in matters
of truft, dealing, or opinion.

I know that there will be perfons infatuated
enough to rely for an exception upon the very
clafs of examples, where, for a hundred reafons,
the rule is likely to hold moft ftrictly. No one,
however, can pretend that a man's fluency goes
any way towards proving his fitnefs for adminifter-
ing public affairs ; and if it do not, where refts the
proof of Mr. Pitt's fitnefs ? What would have
been his confequence, if this fluency had never
caufed him to be diftinguifhed ?

I doubt not but thefe moral and prudential principles *will* be admitted in Mr. Pitt's cafe. But
not, I fear, till, after the rejection of overflowing
evidence, calamity fhall come to fcourge a fro-
ward people into a conviction of their juftnefs.

When Mr. Pitt entered into public life, he
found a Houfe of Commons at war with public
opinion. But as the payment of the intereft of the
funded debt is a nearer and more comprehenfible
good than the purity of one branch of the legif-
lature ; fo the failure of public credit was an evil
much more generally dreaded than an unfaithful re-
prefentation. Mr. Pitt did what was to be done—
ad captandos animos. And thofe whom he difgufted
by his declamations upon the dangerous conftitu-

3   tion

tion of the Houſe of Commons, he conciliated by his homilies upon national thrift. On the ſtrength of plans projected by Lord Shelburne, and of private communications from Dr. Price, he ſet up forthwith for a practitioner in finance ; and it is eaſy to underſtand how, by aſſuming this double part of *financier-reformer*, he would obtain credit both for prudence and, for principle.

Our two-faced idol did not, however, remain long in its original ſtate. The injuries of a few years defaced one of the countenances : the pious credulity of the people taught them to cloſe their eyes when they approached the other ; and till lately they believed that it continued entire.*

We cannot wonder, and it is not worth while to be chagrined, at the obſtinacy of a *paſt* deluſion. In an affair of accompts, very few will

---

* Mr. Burke has ſtooped with the vulgar in adoration of this propitious FISCAL JANUS; but his ſounds like lip-worſhip. Mr. B.'s piety, when heartfelt, is both prolix and fervent. " If any thing defenſive in our domeſtic ſyſtem can ſave " us from the diſaſters of a regicide peace, he (Mr. Pitt) is the " man to ſave us. If the finances, in ſuch a caſe, can be re- " paired, he is the man to repair them." (Reg. Peace, p. 135.) —Mr. Burke is the ableſt poſture-maſter of propoſitions I know. He uſually amuſes his readers and himſelf with placing every opinion, of which he is at the moment convinced, in a variety of attitudes. Here he faintly echoes a popular error.

have

have conftancy to fubmit to a laborious examination of the merits of men and things.

In 1795, foon after a reperufal of the report of
Mr. Pitt's fpeech on his revival of the fcheme of a
finking fund, I met with Mr. S——, a Spanifh
gentleman, a great mafter of the pencil ; I pro-
pofed to him a fubject for the exercife of his art,
fuggefted by a comparifon of the fpeech with the
profpect of public affairs. Soon afterwards he fent
me a neat defign, in which the following are the
principal figures : in the centre ftands a column
ornamented with death's heads, and furrounded by
analagous emblems of difaftrous war, as torn
ftreamers, and broken gun-carriages ; on the right
is a naked and hungry rabble ; on the left, a crowd
of ftock-brokers and monied-intereft men. At
fome diftance ftands a folitary figure fixed in aftonifhment at the infenfibility of this groupe to their
danger from the falling of the broken fhaft, which
is feen inclined towards their fide. The infcription
is as follows : I AM UNCOMMONLY HAPPY TO
FLATTER MYSELF THAT MY NAME MAY BE
INSCRIBED UPON THAT FIRM COLUMN NOW
ABOUT TO BE RAISED TO NATIONAL FAITH
AND NATIONAL PROSPERITY.

I need not *now* expatiate on Mr. Pitt's financial
knowledge, as it has been exhibited with regard
both to Englifh or French affairs. , The events

in

in the two countries have doubly decided his reputation. If his adminiſtration furniſhed no correſponding facts, theſe would determine hiſtorians, in ſumming up his character, to repreſent him as *preſuming* and *ſhallow*.

From the doctrines reſpecting the Houſe of Commons, which he has at different times maintained, we obtain an illuſtration no leſs ſtriking of the *moral* nature of the declaimer. There are inconſiſtencies of opinion, and of conduct, which afford honourable proof of progreſſive wiſdom. But there are alſo inconſiſtencies which no leſs loudly proclaim progreſſive wickedneſs. No inſtance, I believe, of departure from ſolemn profeſſions has made more noiſe in the world than that of the matron of Epheſus. Though leſs renowned, I place beſide it, as equal in degree, the example of Robeſpierre, firſt warmly pleading for the abolition of the puniſhment of death, and afterwards judicially murdering his innocent countrymen and countrywomen by tens, by ſcores, and by hundreds at a time. Not leſs inconſiſtent than either is the man, who, after repeatedly devoting an aſſembly, particularly conſtituted, to the ſuſpicion of his fellow-citizens, and after adjuring them, by their dread of ruinous wars and of oppreſſion, to exert themſelves to alter its conſtitution, ſhall compliment an aſſembly, identical in conſtitution, and undoubtedly comprehended in his denunciation, as

a body

a body in whofe political wifdom and patriotic
virtue it were infatuation or defperate criminality
not to place implicit confidence. What, if he
who, at one time, calls upon you by every private
and public tie to *diflruft*, and at another to *truft*,
fhall have been fo circumftanced as to fpeak, in
the firft cafe, from pure conviction; in the fecond,
from the intereft of his ambition? Shall we af-
cribe his inconfiftency to the improvement of his
underftanding, or the depravation of his heart?

For the Ephefian matron it were eafy to find an
excufe which fome readers would accept as a com-
pleat defence, and others would interpret into a
panegyric. In devoting herfelf to the memory of
her hufband—in forwarding his corpfe to the poft
of infamy, fhe gave herfelf without referve to her
tender feelings. She was a lady of fenfibility.
Amiable fenfibility! who will not pardon the foi-
bles of which thou art the occafion? And how
many would embrace, as a fifter by fentiment, *her*
whom kindnefs of heart betrayed, firft into hafty
vows, and afterwards into too fudden forgetful-
nefs of thofe vows?

As to Robefpierre, the murderer, I leave his
defence, and their own, to the members of that
convention which delayed to wreft from him his
mifufed power. I will, however, in juftice, obferve, that he is not recorded to have brought to a

F   trial

trial of life and death any of thofe who afterwards inculcated the doctrines of fparing humanity with which he fet out, on his way to popularity.

I hope that when Mr. Sheridan, in anfwer to Mr. Pitt (May 7, 1792) afferted, that " neither " in the church, the army, the navy, or any public " office, was any appointment given, but in confe- " quence of parliamentary influence," he was refuted on the fpot, though that is not reported;* or, per- haps, the affertion was confidered as one that might be left to be difcredited by its own notorious falfe. hood. No man ever infifted, like this man, upon the neceffity of the Houfe of Commons having one common intereft and one common feeling with the people. Would he feduce it from its allegiance of fympathy ! he who had fo often declared that the falvation of the country and of individuals from utter ruin depended upon meafures to fecure this legifla- tive body againft complaifance towards a minifter !

On this part of Mr. Pitt's conduct, I leave ge- neral reflections to thofe who have had opportunity of obferving numerous facts. One anecdote I will relate. I have heard a few others of a like nature from the parties principally concerned. When the late Dr. Vanfittart, profeffor of civil law, at Ox- ford, died, the Honourable Dr. W—— happened

---

* New Annual Regifter, 1792, p. 115.

to be in London. He had not, he faid, the fmalleft intention to folicit the appointment; but one morning he was furprifed by a vifit from Mr. Pitt, whofe bufinefs was to offer him the profeffor-fhip. Dr. W—— was a modeft, a well-inftructed, and, above all, a confcientious man. He had never paid attention to the civil law ; and therefore he declined accepting the emolument, till he fhould determine whether he could fubmit to the labour neceffary to a proper difcharge of the truft. Mr. Pitt willingly kept the place vacant till Dr. W—— fhould have formed his refolution ; and took leave, urging the doctor to accept his offer : Dr. W—— did fo, after fome interval ; and he did alfo moft fcrupuloufly perform the conditions which, in his own mind, he had annexed to the acceptation. I know not if there exifted any other perfon of equal connections and equal expectations, in regard to parliamentary intereft, on whom the office could have been conferred. Still lefs can I difcover whether, if Ulpian had been an obfcure and friend-lefs contemporary, Mr. Pitt would have made the fame perfonal application to him in preference to the prefumptive heir to a lord.

On the 27th of June, 1794, a day diftinguifhed by the downfall of Robefpierre, it was remarked, I think, in the Convention, that " men who are " always talking of their own integrity, do not " ceafe to trample that virtue under foot." No

public

public man in our own country, none, perhaps, in
the age in which we live, unlefs it be the tyrant
at whom this obfervation was levelled, has prefumed fo much upon the eafinefs or favourable
prepoffeffions of mankind as Mr. Pitt. None has
fo loudly pronounced the panegyric of his own
probity. In what degree that noblenefs of nature,
which has been fometimes fpoken of as proper to
the foil and climate of Britain, has flourifhed, and
what fruits it has matured under his foftering care,
is not a thing obfcure. We know pretty exactly
how far thofe that have bafked in the fmile of a
ftatefman, who has fo boldly challenged the manly
virtues as his portion, can claim affinity with the
race which ftands characterifed as

" Fierce in their native hardinefs of foul."

We can witnefs whether, within thefe few years,
the ancient Britifh fpirit has beamed from the general eye, or uttered its dictates from the general
tongue. Who has not felt whether or not we have
been fo near reduced to fervility of opinion before
a minifter, that nothing but his follies can have
faved us, if, indeed, we are yet fafe from his
vices? Is it not a circumftance of public notoriety,
whether any one could have called his merits into
queftion without fome hazard of being reviled as a
confpirator, at leaft in will;—a confpirator of a
fpecies, cruel beyond the neceffity of his purpofes
and

and eager to celebrate his fucceffes by a jubilee of
pillage and maffacre?

Mr. Pitt's fpeeches are remarkable from another fingularity, which ought not to be over-
looked by any clafs of men in earneft to know
what reliance they may place upon him. I have not
exactly noticed how many of his exordiums and pe-
rorations confift of a declaration of his feelings.
But I am miftaken if any other of our orators
will be found with fenfibility fo continually in
his mouth. For an example, I refer to the
laft affair of the debts of the Prince of Wales.
Was not this taint of difengenuoufnefs produced
by anxiety to acquire fhewy talents, and fpread
over his whole mind by eafy fuccefs and immode-
rate applaufe?

Nothing in life is more common or copious than
this vein of language: but obferve from what
lips it flows. You will hear it in every circle. In
relating the misfortune of an acquaintance, the
perfons who conceive fuch parade likely to anfwer their purpofe are fure to conclude by trying to
leave with the hearer an impreffion of its effects
upon their own fufceptible nature. " Only think
" what muft have been *my* feelings on the occa-
" fion!"—In whom will you remark this oftenta-
tion of fenfibility? Chiefly, be affured, in the
fwindler, the toad-eater, the legacy-hunter, in
young

young men and maidens eager to fell themfelves
into matrimony with the cripple and the dotard.
Of fuch confifts the tribe that difcharges the dues
of benevolence in words, and deems whatever can
be purchafed by hypocrify *a bargain.* Thofe who
refemble them in plaufibility of demeanour will
feldom be found to differ much from them in infi-
dioufnefs of views.

Many, I am fenfible, will be fcandalized with
this fort of perfonal fcrutiny, on the fcore merely
of politenefs. They will feel it as an infufferable
rudenefs to hint a poffibility of refemblance between thofe bafe-born cheats, who having begun
by courting the people like tribunes, ended by
crufhing them like decemvirs, and our

Memmi clara propago.

But on fo ferious a fubject men of difcernment
will not bring their credulity as an offering to
miftaken good manners. Thefe analogies they
will not either condemn as illiberal, or flight as unwife; nor will they fuffer their prudence to be
amufed by the alledged difficulty of fubftantiating
a charge of duplicity. The cafe here is in no refpect the fame, as when an offence againft fome
criminal law is under inveftigation. The court of
practical common fenfe is not conftituted upon the
principles of a commiffion for gaol-delivery. It
proceeds, and ought to proceed, upon flenderer
proofs :

proofs. But then its penalties reach not the perfon of the convict. The fentences it awards are purely defenfive or negative: its code may be nearly comprized in a fingle precept.

Hic niger eft, hunc tu, Romane, caveto.

Do not give your confidence to fair profeffions, for with fuch do impoftors go abroad. Keep the fufpected at a diftance from your interefts: and, as the confe-quences of fraud are more ruinous, and the temptation ftronger, be quicker of fufpicion in public concerns than in private.

Thofe everlafting harangues of Mr. Pitt which terminated in fo many abortive propofitions for the redrefs of grievances and wrongs, muft have left fome impreffion upon every mind. I am not ab-furd enough to expect that thefe paffages of his life will fimply of themfelves render him an object of averfion to " *people of quality, that are born* " *to great eftates.*" I touch upon them only as proofs of want of will or of ability to accomplifh purpofes which he reprefented as neceffary or juft. The failure is the more ftriking in a minif-ter, who has found unexampled eafe in carrying into effect meafures that had nothing in them of the nature of redrefs: and I fubmit it, whether, in the prefent fituation of things, the augury be encouraging. He who has deceived or difap-pointed one fet of men has, fo far, given no pledge

4   that

that he will not deceive or difappoint another. If
it be true, that fuccefs makes confident, and practice makes perfect, however we may love the
treafon, we have furely caufe to regard the traitor
with diftruft.

But the hiftory of thofe days is as " a tale of
other times." The fchemes that diftinguifhed the
early part of the minifter's public life feem diminu-
tive, as if thrown into diftance by the magnitude of
more recent occurrences. Had Mr. Pitt died fix
years ago, he would have carried with him to the
grave the reputation of being equal to fo trying a
period. The fucceffes of the enemy; the fudden crafh of fo many flourifhing houfes at one
feafon; the deep injury to public credit at another; the late fcarcity ; the prefent want of fpecie;
our bootlefs negotiations for peace ; the profpect
of hoftilities not determinable but in the utter
ruin of the weaker party ; our terrors and difafters
would each, in its turn, have done honour to his
memory. The people would have continually
vifited his tomb in idea ; and paufing over every
circumftance of our afflicted ftate, they would
have faid—*This had never happened, had Mr. Pitt
but lived!*

The hiftorian, as he could not, like the contemporary vulgar, be fafcinated by illufions in-
feparable from the perfon of the Minifter, would
have

have found in Mr. Pitt's career, had it closed in
1792, subject for ridicule instead of regret. Pro-
testations of devotion to the people have been
much too regularly succeeded by encroachments
on popular rights, and aggravations of public burdens, to leave us in any uncertainty about their
value. In the suppofed cafe, however, must not
the deaf and blind fury of the British cabinet have
infallibly led an unbiaffed thinker to a speculation
of the following tendency? " We have followed
" the continental despots in their first movements;
" and we have seen that ' *the Wonder of the Isle* '
" had not genius and magnanimity to avail him-
" felf of that cheap opportunity to exalt his coun-
" try above all ancient and all modern fame.
" Nevertheless, we may presume that a return of
" his early parliamentary feelings would have pre-
" vented him from persisting, with the insanity of
" his successors, to set all the forces of the physi-
" cal and moral world at defiance. If he had
" not altogether avoided a perilous contest, he
" would have terminated it, while yet he could dic-
" tate the conditions of peace. That astonishing
" reverse in the *internal* situation of the belligerent
" powers took place by gradations too palpable to
" escape ordinary penetration. And for a confi-
" derable period, it was not much more difficult
" to stop than to detect the progress of ruin.
" His country, therefore, has, it must be con-
" feffed, abundant caufe to lament the premature

G   " lofs

" lofs of the only member of her councils, in
" favour of whofe capacity there were any fpecious
" appearances, or whofe incapacity had not been
" evinced by the experience of a fimilar crifis."
To him, who has traced to its formation, or de-
duced from his conduct, the falfe and hollow character of the minifter, it cannot be obfcure why he
has thus difgraced all conjecture. Spoiled child
of unruffled profperity! he could eafily extract out
of circumftances an apology to himfelf for mifcar-
riage in his Ruffian adventure. The reft was all
calculated to fill him with a perfuafion, that he
fhould not find in his opponents more fenfe than
in his admirers, or more fpirit than in his tools.

However ftrenuoufly it may be denied, that a
depraved heart, elated by the ready fuccefs of
thofe artifices by which he has managed for a
feafon to exalt himfelf and degrade his rivals, fur-
nifhes the clue to Mr. Pitt's recent conduct, one
truth muft be admitted. That OUR MISFORTUNES
SPRING FROM THE ROOT OF FATALLY FALSE
VIEWS ftands clear of all precarioufnefs of rea-
f   cerning motives. We have been led,
        after campaign, from error to error,
1. .. one difappointment to another. After tracing
the thorny maze till we are faint with labour and
lofs of blood, we find ourfelves farther from the
goal than at fetting out. It was to the humilia-
tion of the enemy, if not to the difmemberment of
                                                his

his territory, that we at firſt looked forward. We have ſeen the baſe of that enemy's power extended by additions more than equal to a moderate ſtate; and does not his fame in arms, at this moment, tranſcend his high traditionary renown?* Such has been the reſult of our military ſchemes.—We have tried pacific overtures; and they, in conformity to the ſame rule, have ſerved but to rekindle his flagging animoſity. *Such* facts deſerve the moſt ſcrupulous examination. Their connection and bearings may enable us to comprehend how far an adminiſtration, whoſe conduct is made up of theſe diſaſtrous riddles, can be our ſtrength in war, or our ſafeguard in peace.

For unfolding the character of our formidable adverſary, there are other good reaſons beſides the purpoſe of a compariſon with the conceptions of miniſtry. I preſume to think that it has been entirely miſconceived by a politician, ſuperior to Mr. Pitt in the philoſophy of hiſtory by as many degrees as he may be inferior in the practice of intrigue. His eloquent miſſtatements doubtleſs quickened the general eagerneſs of the great to join the miniſter. May not the ſame cauſe ſtill operate to prevent them from deſerting ſo dangerous a leader?

---

* Ingentes GALLORUM glorias.——*Tacitus.*

In

In moſt of the tranſactions which hiſtory records, the people are paſſive inſtruments in the hands of a few individuals, in whom, not only the national peculiarities, but the general traces of humanity, are pretty well obliterated. It may, therefore, be the more difficult to aſcertain the qualities that predominate at large in the different maſſes of mankind. Among the few inſtances, however, in which they are prominent and eaſy to be aſcertained the preſent is to be numbered.

While the repulſive genius of the feudal ariſto-cracy operated in full force upon other regions, the component parts of France were drawn into a degree of union, and pervaded by a common feel-ing. This as yet rude and imperfectly animated whole, the romantic or ſatyrical ſtrains of the Troubadours and the Courts of Love, ſeem to have informed with new life, and to have impreſſed with an indelible character.* The mind of the people, we are certain, was wrought, centuries ago, to a very lofty pitch, and if it ever ſuffered depreſſion, it ſoon mounted up again to its ſtand-ard elevation. By degrees, was formed that habit of enthuſiaſm, in which lies the ſtrength and weak-neſs, the good and evil of the French character. Hence the readineſs to fly out beyond the limits within which other nations reſtrain both their feel-

* See Mr.Woltman's Hiſt. Eſſay on this ſubject, in Schiller's Horen. for 1795, St. 5.

ings

ings and the expreffion of thofe feelings. Hence
excefs of ferocity and excefs of frivolity, vifulence
of rancour, and womanifhnefs of fympathy. Hence
centaur compounds of the mountebank and the
knight-errant; and the *ape* and *tyger* traits, noticed
by VOLTAIRE. To each horrid barbarity, each
heroic exploit, each ludicrous fpectacle, exhibited
during the troubles of our time, a parallel may be
quoted from the annals of every one of the laft
twenty generations. The crufades and chivalry
fhew this people always foremoft in adventure.
Scarce one of their numerous wars but has had its
Amazons. Even modern difcipline cannot rein
in the headlong heroifm of individuals. How
often have privates, officers, and generals, during the prefent conteft, rufhed forward fingly to
encounter the worft hazards of battle! and how
many thoufand champions *without fear and without
reproach* have rallied round the cradle of freedom!
To this hour the hiftory of Joan of Arc retains
fomething of a fupernatural air. Yet Joan only
united the powers of a religious miracle and a
maiden hero. Her appearance was but an expe-
riment of the effects of gallantry and fanaticifm on
a nation, of which we know that, by other incen-
tives, it may be roufed in a mafs, with equal ardour, to expel an invader from its foil. In the
conduct of their fuperiors at a former period, the
poiffardes had a precedent for their difgufting in-
humanity on the day of the Thuilleries. The
ladies

ladies of the court were feen, on the morrow of
St. Bartholomew, to flock in groups round the
murdered nobles, with whom they had been lately
coquetting; and they were heard to jeft upon the
appearance of the corpfes !

The writer, on whofe authority we, on this fide
the water, have been generally content to take up
our ideas of Jacobinifm, is fond of enlarging on
certain recent exhibitions at Paris. " No mecha-
" nical means," he obferves, " could be devifed
" in favour of this incredible fyftem of wickednefs
" that has not been employed."—" All forts of
" fhews and exhibitions, calculated to inflame and
" vitiate the imagination and pervert the moral fenfe,
" have been contrived."—" In mockery of all reli-
" gion, they inftitute impious, blafphemous, in-
" decent, theatric rites, in honour of their vitiated
" perverted reafon, and erect altars to the perfo-
" nification of their own corrupted and bloody
" republic." *Burke's Reg. Peace, pp.* 99, 100.

In other paffages and pamphlets the author has
more in the fame ftile. But he ought to have
known, and knowing, he ought to have told that
thefe are no devices of the " new French legif-
" lators." They have defcended in a right line
from loyalty and fuperftition to republicanifm and
infidelity. Thefe fhapes and fcenes have ever been
the joy of an ingenious people. Their lively fancy
has

as been accuſtomed, from the dark ages down-
wards, to diſplay itſelf in extravagancies of a taſte
equally vile.

Early in the fourteenth century the ſtreets of
Paris were ſtrewed and illuminated for a ſpectacle,
of which a full deſcription would be too ſhocking,
even for the lax piety of this age. The Son of God
was ſhewn in one place, raiſing and judging the
dead; in another, ſaying the Lord's Prayer with
his diſciples; in a third, eating ſugar-plums and at
play with his mother. You had beſides heaven
and hell; Adam and Eve, in their ſtate of inno-
cence; here, a herd of ſavages fighting over their
victuals; there, courtezans diſplaying their ſeductive
arts. As an accompaniment to all this, a fox was
exhibited; firſt, in the garb of an undignified di-
vine, then as biſhop, afterwards as archbiſhop,
and laſtly, in the attire of the holy father himſelf.
The reaſon for each ſucceſſive advance is the greater
and greater havoc he makes among the pullets.—
But a religious ſolemnity, long and generally celebrated in France, defeats the whole claim of
Mr. Burke's Jacobin proceſſions to originality. In
commemoration of the flight of the Virgin Mary
into Egypt, the moſt beautiful damſel of the place,
clad in coſtly attire, was mounted upon a richly
capariſoned aſs. This captivating repreſentative
of the mother of the Meſſiah was attended by the
clergy and people to the metropolitan church. It

I   is is not to my purpofe to relate how the congregation, inftead of faying Amen, exerted themfelves to bray, and how much their devotion was enlivened if the afs founded a genuine note. But it is clear, that perfonifications of abftract entities by nature's ftatuary are no Jacobin inventions, but mere " antique pageantries." And if *the age of chivalry be paft*, the enthufiafm of the age of chivalry has not been extinguifhed. The fubjects of a monarchy loft, as we have felt, nothing of their ardour by being tranfmuted into citizens of a republic. It is true, ten thoufand fwords were no longer ready to leap out of the fcabbard to avenge a look rudely caft on a beautiful and high-born dame. The chivalry of the wearers was, in this inftance, tempered by their moral feelings. They had been taught (I know not whether by calumnious rumours) that fhe was an habitual violator of allher public and all her private duties. Liberty, however, acquired more votaries than Beauty loft. And no fooner was infult offered to this new object of adoration, than there

—————————— outflew
Millions of flaming fwords.

An alteration in its application is no proof that a power is loft or impaired. A miftrefs may be abandoned without detriment to the amorous propenfity. We every day fee individuals exerting
equal

equal ardour in the moſt oppoſite purſuits. If that
abject devotion to kings, for which the French
were ſo long the contempt of Engliſhmen, has
been renounced,

> And Seine, no more obſequious as he runs,
> Pour at GREAT BOURBON's feet his ſilken ſons;

ſuch change of inclination does not prove that the
actuating principle of the French character is de-
ſtroyed.

Loyalty conſiſts in attachment to particular political inſtitutions, united with a reverential regard
for thoſe who exerciſe the higheſt functions of
government. The grand law * of the drama holds
in this, as it does in many other ſituations of real
life. The unſeen dead letter little moves the populace. The living perſonage, by appealing to
ſenſe, gains entire poſſeſſion of the fancy. The
affections eaſily make a ſecond tranſition; and
loyalty exhibits itſelf not leſs in humouring the
caprices of the man than in honouring the authority of the magiſtrate. Courtiers and prieſts do
not fail to encourage this diſpoſition: greedy of
preſent favour and the rewards of favour, they

---

* Segniùs irritant animos demiſſa per aurem,
  Quam quæ ſunt oculis ſubjecta fidelibus—

think

think or care little about the danger in which their officious flattery is involving their patron.

What is proverbially faid of charity applies to loyalty. If this fentiment be to abide the fhocks of time and chance, *it fhould begin at home.* You ought to find, by your own firefide, reafons for fatisfaction with that form of fociety to which you belong. With every other fashion of loyalty, natural affection wages an eternal war; and, fooner or later, will fhe gain a terrible victory. It is a forced and precarious ftate, when a man is cajoled to feek his own happinefs in the feelings of another. We have witneffed in our day the effects of this immoral and impious ftrain of hypocrify. How much better had it been for the race of Capet, if the people of France had never been fo funk in political fuperftition as to offer up themfelves and their children to every whim of glory and ambition that happened to enter into the heart of their fovereign! I doubt not, but an indignant fenfe of the grofs adulation, paid by his forefathers to Louis XIV. has embittered many a Frenchman againft Louis XVI. Nothing is more common than this unjuft transfer of revenge; and our feelings, when new, are conftantly apt to run into excefs. Among the recent converts to Chriftianity, none treated the ftatues of Jupiter with fo much indignity as thofe who had been the moft devout Pagans. And, at the Reformation, perfecution was drawn down upon many an unoffending papift, by deteftation of the fuccefsful frauds of the old agents of popery.

Upon this ftatement I appeal to the reader's prudential feelings. To the cafe of a people, born with a temperament fo fanguine, and placed in circumftances more irritating than thofe which converted Dutch and American phlegm into fire, how would he apply the maxims by which he regulates his actions? None but a lunatic or an ideot would adopt the ftile of the negro-driver, who is brandifhing the whip over a recovered runaway flave. The negro-driver himfelf would not let his vengeance fo freely loofe, if he fuppofed there was the leaft chance of his fcurrility and violence being retorted. Nor is there any human motive for the conduct of the Britifh miniftry, but an affurance of the fame kind. That they felt confident of having the enemy completely at their mercy, is pofitively proved by their repeated affertions. Of thefe affertions, which occur in a variety of fpeeches, and in public papers, Lord Auckland's hectoring declaration,* with the juftificative comments of Lord

Grenville

---

* " Some of thefe deteftable regicides are now in fuch a
" fituation *that they can be fubjected to the fword of the law.*
" The reft are ftill in the midft of a people whom they have
" plunged into an abyfs of evils, and for whom famine, anar-
" chy, and civil war, are about to prepare new calamities. In

" fhort

Grenville and Mr. Pitt, forms the moſt curious repoſitory. Mr. Dundas, whom neither the general effect of years nor ſpecial experience could render wary, chimes in with the ſtupid and inſolent temerity of his aſſociates. The war *muſt*, he is certain, be *ſucceſsful* and *glorious*.* They did not truſt to menaces alone. In the true taſte of politicians of their leaven, they held forth lures which, to a nation that felt its right and its power to give itſelf a government, muſt have been a thouſand times more provoking than all their abuſe. It deſerves remark, that the very ſame clumſy combination of expedients had been tried in the laſt war. Lord Hood's proclamation, melted into a maſs with Lord Auckland's declaration, would form exactly ſuch an alloy as that by which William Eden, Eſq. and his fellow commiſſioners, operated upon the hopes and fears of America. Neither ſet of theſe notable political magnetiſers could bring on the deſired criſis; their ſubjects wanted faith. The one nation was as incredulous to the "*ſenſibility of the coaleſced powers to its dreadful* "*ſituation*," as the other to that "*benevolence of* "*Great Britain which checked the extremes of war*,

---

"ſhort, every thing that we ſee happen induces us to confiden "*as not far diſtant the end of theſe wretches.*" &c. April 5, 1793. See alſo Debrett's Lords Debates of June 17, and Commons Debates of April 25, 1793.

* Debates, December 19, 1793.

"*rather*

" *rather than diſtreſs a people ſtill conſidered as fellow-*
" *ſubjects.*" I do not recollect whether the ſchool
treatiſes of oratory furniſh a ſcale of inſults. But
ſurely the perſons, whoſe *inſtructions* * could ſug-
geſt ſuch compoſitions, might, by ſome chance,
have learned that there are natures which nothing
ſtings ſo much as the arrogance of pity.

The abſurdity of attempting to ſubdue a lofty-
ſpirited people, by the brute diſcipline of ſtripes
and ſops, is now felt by thoſe who could not an-
ticipate it. Of this ſcheme of policy the conſequences are not leſs important than obvious. Can
it be a queſtion, whether one, ſo incapable as Mr.
Pitt has proved himſelf of entering into the ſtrongeſt
feelings of human beings, is fit to regulate their
moſt important relations? Or, are the feelings of
individuals no longer the ſprings of ſociety? And
do we in no wiſe riſque the diſorder of the vaſt
machine, by entruſting it to the hands of a man,
unacquainted with the force and bearing of its
moving powers?—I aſſume, that the rich now deſire
peace from apprehenſion as ardently as the poor
have long deſired it from ſuffering. What then is
the deſcription of the miniſter, under whoſe auſpices
the negotiators would meet with the *leaſt* chance of

---

* Lord Grenville is ſtated to have ſaid, that Lord Auckland's
declaration was in the ſpirit of his inſtructions, though not in
the letter. June 17, 1793.

accom-

accomplishing their object ? Is it not of him whose foul-mouthed invectives have been reinforced by a feries of public papers, which, "taken to-
" gether, convey no distinct idea, except that of
" extending absolute power, and encouraging
" unlimited monarchy ?"* Is it not of him, who to one of the parties that are to contract has become lefs detectable only as he became more contemptible ? Without doubt, then, it must be obvious to common fenfe, that anxiety to remove such an obstacle to pacification is the only fure token of a difpofition to extricate ourfelves from the distreffes and hazards of war.

But the obstacle in question is alfo an obstacle in a fenfe totally distinct from the mere procefs of negotiation. Whoever poffeffes the ufeful talent of tranfporting himfelf by imagination into the track of other men's thoughts, must become fenfible, that *the prefent minifter is the grand reliance of the enemy*; and, confequently, that his difgrace

* Marquis of Lanfdowne, Feb. 17, 1794. Some paffages in the papers are categorical enough, as to the intention of impofing a government upon France ; and by thefe the French would fix the fenfe of the reft. " They (the coalefced powers) " fee no other remedy but the re-eftablifhment of the French " monarchy. *It is for this*, and the acts of aggreffion com- " mitted by the executive power of France, that *we* have " armed, in conjunction with other powers." *Lord Hood, Aug.* 23, 1793.

would make a ftronger impreffion in our favour than the moft vigorous military preparations. Can we flatter ourfelves that the depreffion of Great Britain, and the concomitant elevation of her rival, have proceeded at a rate fo flow, and from caufes fo obfcure as to efcape the Directory? Has not that body the fagacity to connect our Weft India expeditions,* and our fubfidies, with the confifcation of the fpecie due to the creditors of our bank? Cannot they trace the laft calamity to the crude conceptions of one overweening mind? Do they not confider it as the fure forerunner of others fimilar? Are they not looking with confident expectation to the moment when England fhall be rendered fo fick at heart that life fhall fpontaneoufly defert her extremities? Have they not the fecurity of direct experience, that the war cannot long be continued by *its prefent conductors* without our dependencies either dropping off at the leaft touch of violence, or draining the mother-country into a ftate of irremediable exhauftion? In retaliating imitation of an adverfary's councils, they may be more intent upon the ruin of England than the welfare of France; and, although I do not take the refult of Lord Malmefbury's miffion to be any teft of their feelings, I have confidered

---

* See Mr. Burke's additional half-fheet of bitter, but juft, invective againft our expenfive acquifition of thefe expenfive " tropical cemeteries." *Reg. Peace.*

them

them as utterly indifpofed to treat with Mr. Pitt, ever fince they have felt fecure at home. The fubfequent rapid amelioration in the condition of France might well induce them to oblige our minifter to take time to confummate the work in which he had vifibly advanced fo far. Upon this fpeculation is it improbable they will refufe *him* the terms they would concede to any other man ? I fay *any other man,* fuppofing that, in the eye both of the enemy and of the byftanding nations, he muft rank among the moft defpicable of politicians. And I propofe my conjecture to his powerful patrons, becaufe I fufpect, that fooner than abandon his poft he would prove falfe to both parts of his nature, and *fincerely* negotiate *upon his knees.* What, though he fhould lick the duft from the feet of regicides, whom he has been thefe five years vilifying? has not his tongue already been employed in offices as oppofite ?

I obferve further, that, on any fcheme, the prefent minifter muft henceforth labour under a peculiar and a moft ferious difadvantage. For he has miftaken the Englifh no lefs than the French *
character.

---

* I have only fhewn how grofsly he miftook the *fpirit* of the French. He equally mifcalculated their *means* and their *intelligence.* Of his wild errors concerning the effect of the depreciation of affignats, the theme of fo many puffy orations, the whole world is fully apprifed. "We went about afking when affignats

character. He muft have fancied that we fhould
hold ourfelves bound to him, whatever might be-
tide, for better and for worfe; and that we fhould

"fignats would expire, and we laughed at the laft price of them.
"But what fignified the fate of thofe tickets?" In fuch a conteft, every man, undebauched by intrigue, muft have felt that
the indications of conduct were not to be taken from the credit
of paper-money, but the pulfes of the foul. I fhould fuppofe
many coal-heavers were inftinctively certain that the enemy
would not give up refiftance till they experienced an almoft total
failure

Of man and fteel, the foldier and his fword.

It is, in my mind, quite natural that a ftatefman who looks but
to the revenue for the ftate of the body politic, and at the revenue but with the eye of an excifeman, fhould commit errors
which a coal-heaver would have avoided.

The temporary fuccefs of Mr. Pitt's practices at home might
make him conceit he could produce fimilar effects by fimilar
means abroad. But the French were deaf to his lamentations
over their evils, and his offers to apply a remedy. They
fpurned with high difdain the εχθρων αδωρα δωρα. Nor would
they be content to take what they endured from aggreffion, and
from domeftic tyrants whom aggreffion raifed to power, for an
effect of liberty. The fcheme of fickening the French of liberty,
like all the reft, produced an effect contrary to what the pro-
jector intended. It only animated them with fiercer indignation
againft thofe who intermeddled in their affairs. Upon the merit
or demerit of their fortitude, I appeal to the opinion that fhall
prevail through Europe in 1800. To their dreadful provifional
fufferings they were, doubtlefs, not lefs fenfible than the pack
of Britifh orators. But from the dreary wildernefs of anarchy,
they would not be driven back to the refuge of their old
Egyptian bondage. By pufhing forward they hoped to emerge
into the land of promife.

I   never

never dream of fuing for a divorce. But, as is ufual with perfons of his clafs, he has undeceived by deeds thofe whom he had deceived by words. Nor will an opinion, reluctantly formed upon clofe acquaintance, be haftily difmiffed.

It has been juftly obferved by Mr. Burke, that " no war *can* long be carried on againft the will of " the people," and that " this war in particular " cannot be carried on unlefs they are enthu- " fiaftically in favour of it." (*Reg. Peace*, p. 65.) Whether the people are fobered out of their enthu- fiafm is now no longer, I hope, a queftion. But whatever may be their feelings towards any meafure, diflike to the minifter who is to carry it into effect, would choak enthufiafm in its birth. Here then is a political *ftudy* for thofe who have adhered to Mr. Pitt as their temporal faviour—an unpopular war, an obnoxious minifter, an enemy that has waxed ftronger in the ftruggle, a difficulty (ap- proaching to an impoffibility) of fupplies, a ftate of public credit, commerce, manufactures, and probably of revenue, fuch as threatens a privation of *artificial* refources, and a country comparatively weak in *natural* means of carrying on a great and coftly war. Hiftory does not furnifh the iffue of fuch a crifis. But can prudence draw no inftruction from the nature of things? I am much deceived if it be not the clear anfwer of this unerring oracle, that Mr. Pitt cannot force forward without danger

of

of overthrowing fociety at every ftep. What ! will not new burdens, frefh vexations, diftrefs increafing, and *his* adminiftration prolonged, four more and more the public temper ? Will not difcontent grow more and more importunate ? Will not he oppofe to this annoyance rigourous laws and fevere exertions of authority ? The probable or poffible termination of this action and re-action, I leave to the opulent to confider, fincerely wifhing their timely exertions may prevent what otherwife the chroniclers of Mr. Pitt's revolutionary career might have to record. One of his flatterers has fuggefted to him the defperate confolation of a monument of ruins. I know not whether this, intentionally or unintentionally, will be his end. But I am fure that neither the enemy, nor neutral nations, nor unborn ages, will wafte a fingle figh over his fate.

No point in politics was ever more warmly contefted, and none has been more perfectly fettled than the credit due to Lord North's public talents. This uniformity of opinion feems deferving of the attention of that clafs to whom I addrefs thefe reflections. Lord North may ferve as an eafy and exact ftandard of comparifon for Mr. Pitt. Had his Lordfhip been effectually and feafonably employed in this capacity, his memory would perhaps have been more ufeful to his country than his life was injurious. I will try if he can now be turned to any account.

1. Twenty

1. Twenty years ago, it was *who but Lord North ?*

1. Till lately, it was *who but Mr. Pitt ?*—Pitt for ever!

2. In Lord North's time, as long as peace was preferved, the poor laboured, the rich traded, and the nation profpered.

2. In Mr. Pitt's time, as long as peace was preferved, the poor laboured, the rich traded, and the country profpered.

To what, in both cafes, was the national profperity owing? To what but the induftry, enterprize, and genius of individuals, unmolefted by this wild and wafteful work of war. Had thefe minifters been both roaming the deferts of Grand Tartary all their lives, our profperity would have been juft the fame, fo we had had juft as much peace. The bufinefs of commercial treaties and regulations would have been tranfacted full as well by others as by Mr. Pitt. But what other minifter would have prefumed to ftand forward as the creator of our profperity; or what other would have failed to be fcouted as a fhamelefs charlatan? *he* who did lefs by his fpeeches and fchemes towards the promotion of trade, than one fingle water-wheel by its revolutions!

3. Lord

3. Lord North was unimpeachable in his domeftic relations.

3. Mr. Pitt, for what I know, is fo too. ' Of his fraternal affection, a certain blufhing book once bore an unequivocal proof. This fact alone is decifive of his public integrity.

4. How did our lords and ladies, our fquires and dames, our yeomanry and commonalty, once join in full chorus to Lord North, as a man of bufinefs, a capital orator, and an incomparable financier! How many thoufand wretches paid with life and limb for this full-mouthed folly!

4. And Mr. Pitt is fuch a man of bufinefs, fuch an orator! *fuch* a financier! that, heaven forgive our ingratitude, we have almoft forgotten his noble predeceffor. Doubtlefs, to take money out of the people's pocket, while it contains any, is an admirable feat for a man who has the law for his clutch. The late King of Pruffia ufed to define an Englifh general, *any man you pleafe in a blue coat faced with red.* And an Englifh financier his Majefty might have defined—*any man who can propofe heavy taxes in a long fpeech,*

5. During peace Lord North paid off about ten millions of the national debt. In eight years of

war

war he added ten pounds for every pound he took off.

5. During peace Mr. Pitt paid off some twenty millions. In five years of war he has added six or eight pounds for every pound he took off.

6. Lord North's helpmates were Dundas, Jenkinson, Wedderburne, with some others now dead.

6. Who are Mr. Pitt's helpmates? The same Dundas, the same Jenkinson, the same Wedderburne. Were the rest alive, they would, I doubt not, give Mr. Pitt as effectual aid to overcome the French, as they did Lord North to overcome the Americans.

7. This campaign, and that campaign, the Americans, we were told, were to be brought to our feet.

7. In like manner, according to Mr. Pitt, the French were at their last gasp any time for three whole years. At one period they were to be famished to death. Then atrophy, the paper-palsy, and convulsions were, each in turn, to be their end. Alas! that Political Foresight should so rarely have had lodgings in Downing-street!

8. Last war,

8. And this war, the British navy has upheld

its

its ancient fame. Next war, whether wife men or fools are at the helm, the national fong will be

Rule, Britannia, rule the waves.

9. Lord North let flip every opportunity for putting an end to bloodfhed. He repeatedly offered what, fome months fooner, would have been accepted.

9. The moft glorious opportunity that ever occurred to mortal man for compofing the troubles of the world prefented itfelf to Mr. Pitt! and he was folicited to embrace it! He has gone on, adding neglect to neglect, and how dear will he have made his country buy the hard conditions fhe muft at laft receive!

10. Neither Lord North,

10. Nor Mr. Pitt underftood, nor would they ever learn, with whom they had to deal. On what occafion was either tried, and did not fail, unlefs when it was expedient to make a cajoling fpeech?

11. What the better were the needy and the miferable for Lo d North?

11. How

11. How many poor men—*honeſt*, poor men— ever profited by any ſcheme of Mr. Pitt's ? From 1784 to 1792 the wretchedneſs of the poor went on uniformly increaſing, and as faſt, at leaſt, as the exports and imports. Compare this with Mr. Pitt's eternal profeſſions ; and if you have a ſenſe for human wickedneſs and woe, your firſt feeling will be impatience for dead and living nature to come and help you to curſe.

12. Our fathers ! your ſons call upon you, in the name of common ſenſe, and by the irreparable evils your credulity has entailed upon poſterity, to declare why, at the commencement and during the progreſs of the American war, you put confidence in Lord North.

12. Deſirous of an individual's ſhare in the welfare, and not in the calamities of my country, I wiſhed, five years ago, that the firſt boy, from the neareſt blue ſchool, ſhould be miniſter of the country rather than Mr. Pitt. I am miſtaken if thoſe who refer to the true teſt of a miniſter's merit, the domeſtic condition of the whole people, can condemn this wiſh, as contrary to prudence or patriotiſm.

13. Lord North never inſtigated the people to contempt of one branch of the legiſlature, as then conſtituted. Lord North never recommended it

to the people " to affemble in diftricts, becaufe it
" was in vain to look to parliament for a regene-
" ration originating within itfelf." Lord North,
after teaching that nothing honeft was to be expected
from a certain body, did never infift that the deareft
interefts of mankind might be fafely committed to
that body. Lord North never attempted to cement
the fyftem of borough-monging by ————————.

13. ▬ ▬ ▬ ▬ ▬
▬ ▬ ▬ ▬ ▬ ▬

14. Lord North did never boaft of having
placed public credit on a rock, and afterwards
bring the eftablifhment upon which public credit
depends to ftop payment.

14. ▬ ▬ ▬ ▬ ▬
▬ ▬ ▬ ▬ ▬

15. Lord North never called down " the indignation of a great fuffering people," and " the vengeance of the Almighty upon the heads" of certain
perfons, and afterwards joined all that were left
alive of the fame junto in a fyftem, fimilarly, but
far more fweepingly deftructive than that in which
he charged them with the guilt of being engaged.

15. ▬ ▬ ▬ ▬ ▬
▬ ▬ ▬ ▬ ▬ ▬ ▬

In

In addition to this parallel, which I have endeavoured to form on juft and pertinent grounds of refemblance, I fhall addrefs a few queftions to the prudence of the rich minifterialifts.*

Did ever minifter, in a country where the right of expreffing an opinion on public affairs was acknowledged, proceed through fuch a courfe as Mr. Pitt's five laft years with fo little interruption ?

Is it lefs evident that he ftands fully condemned by a vaft majority of the middling and lower claffes, than that he has had free fcope to work out his own damnation ?

By what poffible motives, in oppofition to fenfe and feeling, can this multitude be reclaimed to confidence in Mr. Pitt ?

* I am by no means infenfible to the merit of the enlightened opponents of the minifter among the opulent and the noble. But as their efforts have produced no apparent effect, I have all along confidered the infatuation of the majority as the infatuation of the whole. To a perfon not aware that ignorance will always mifjudge, it muft feem unaccountable that the honour of the wife and the benefit refulting from their counfels fhould be alike *pofthumous*—that a North and a Pitt fhould, for a feafon, have more influence, even with the devoted populace, than a Shelburne or a Fox, a Dundas than a Grey, a Jenkinfon than a Lauderdale, a Wedderburne than a Dunning, a Wilberforce than a Saville.

Would

Would a violent fuppreffion of difcontent be practicable ? would it be fafe ?

May not the great lofe much more by the confequences of a diftraction of public fentiment, than they can gain from minifterial bounty ?

Did they conceive it poffible that the adverfity of April, 1797, could have followed fo clofe upon the profperity of April, 1792 ?

In a long and intricate fuit of law, would they truft a folicitor, who had mifmanaged all the firft proceedings, with its further profecution ? Or would they feel this as an irrefiftible motive for putting the affair into other hands ?

How could French wickednefs be an excufe for Englifh folly ?

Would they have been guided by Mr. Pitt, if they had forefeen that he would have reduced us to our prefent ftate ?

Would they have acquiefced in each and all of the following meafures :

In the refufal to interpofe, on account of a punctilio, at the requeft of Louis XVI. between the German defpots and France ?

In

In the haughty difmiffal of M. Chauvelin ?

In negativing Mr. Fox's motion for fending a minifter to Paris ?

In refufing to receive M. Maret ?

In inattention to M. le Brun's almoft fupplicating letters ?

In not concluding a glorious peace after the cap-ture of Valenciennes ?

In Mr. Pitt's neglecting fo many opportunities of fecuring immortal honour and ineftimable ad-vantages to his country, and that probably from ideas of conqueft fcarce confiftent with fanity ?

In his not acknowledging the republic when all internal commotions were fubdued ?

In leaving the object of the war in perpetual obfcurity, and the contradictory mafs of declara-tions without a full explanation ; in confequence of which the enemy muft impute to us the utmoft malignity of intention ?

In Lord Malmefbury's not carrying our ultima-tum with him to Paris ?

In

In infifting on the reftoration of Belgium as an *indifpenfable* preliminary to peace, when we had no probable means of enforcing the condition ?

In delaying to make the beft peace that could be made at the time being, till the coalition was finally diffolved ?

In that imbecility which feconded the long obvious defign of referving Britain for full and final vengeance ?

Do the rich minifterialifts really look upon the ftate-pilot, who, in defiance of unceafing remonftrances and of the moft evident appearances—*projecit patriam*—has perfilted in running his country on the breakers, the fitteft perfon to fteer us back into calm water ?

If not, why do they not unite immediately with the people in all legal endeavours to remove him from the helm ?

Do they think Mr. Pitt more truft-worthy becaufe he has been always furrounded by a little groupe of pietifts? Do they not know that the moft bloody of tyrants hal the cant, and the leer of a modern faint ? * Do they fuppofe the

---

* Il (Robefpierre) fe fait une reputation d'aufterité qui vife à la fainteté. Il monte fur les bancs. Il parle de Dieu et de providence.——Cromwell's cafe is well known.

people

people ignorant that fraud is oftener found under a religious maſk than grace? And are not the orgies of the late Shrewſbury election, a proof that methodiſm is no ſafeguard againſt the loweſt of the political paſſions?

Are the miniſter's well-wiſhers held in ſuſpenſe by compaſſion? Doubtleſs this ſentiment will affect every thinking mind. When I conſider Mr. Pitt *abſtractedly*, and compare what he is with what a wife and uncorrupt man in his ſituation would have been, he fills me with deep commiſeration. But I alſo feel the ſame ſorrowful emotions when I regard the being, whom ſome critics take to be the hero of Paradiſe Loſt, as alone in the univerſe. Beſides, it is often an act of the moſt ſincere friendſhip to force a man from a ſituation in which he has diſgraced himſelf. And I am ſure Mr. Pitt would be much more the object of compaſſion, and much leſs of hatred, in retirement than in power,

APPENDIX.

APPENDIX.

A GREAT majority, I believe, of the well-informed and truly independent perſons in Great Britain fully anticipated the deplorable conſequences of the war. Early in 1792, I well remember the following lines ad-hering to my memory with that tormenting pertinacity which I have noticed in imperfect febrile delirium :

> " O alienate from truth ! O ſpirit accurſed !
> " Forſaken of all good ! I ſee thy fall
> " Determin'd, and thy hapleſs crew involv'd
> " In this perfidious fraud—contagion ſpread,
> " Both of thy crime and puniſhment."

The practices going buſily forward at the end of the ſummer, 1792, induced me _then_ to publiſh a warning to the people not to be ſeduced.—I cannot diſcern the unex-preſſed wiſhes of the heart. But if I had been miniſter, and deſirous of _getting up an inclination to war_ with France, I would have had that done which Mr. Pitt's adherents and perſonal friends actually did. I would have

4   fired

fired the people, by appeals to their compaſſion, till they
had loſt all fenſe and care of their own fafety—The people
were maddened ; and what was ſaid to bring them back to
their perfect mind merely rendered them outrageous againſt
their faithful and prudent adviſers. Such was the effect
of the publication above-mentioned, from which I ſhall
copy a few ſentences. They will ſhew what apprehenſions
I entertained at that early period. " A paper, ſoliciting
" fubſcriptions for the relief of French refugees, and
" ſigned by ſeveral reſpectable names—H. E. Monckton
" —J. H. Browne, Eſq. MM. PP.—Rev. J. C. Wood-
" houſe, Hordern, Molineux, and Biſhton, W. B.
" Taylor—is at preſent in circulation. Benevolence is
" doubtleſs a fine quality ; but benevolence, when blind,
" becomes, at leaſt, uſeleſs ; and when bigotted, it is
" pernicious. For the ferment of bigotry can convert
" charity into uncharitableneſs."

" If it had been intended to inflame the people of
" England to the thirſt of blood againſt the French, a
" more artful method" (than by ſuch addreſſes) "could not
" have been deviſed. Both with reſpect to the diſtreſs
" of the refugees, and the wickedneſs which has reduced
" them to diſtreſs, full ſcope is left to the imagination.
" And the cauſes of their diſtreſs, conſcience and reli-
" gion, are the moſt affecting you could chooſe. I do
" not charge the promoters of charity with a deſign to
" promote blood-ſhed indirectly. But the vague, am-
" biguous phraſes they have ſcattered abroad have ma-
" nifeſtly ſuch a tendency. It was one of the arts by
" which the ſpirits of the people were kept up during
" the attack upon America.—It was the way in which
" the Birmingham riots were raiſed. It is the way in
                                                            which

" which wholefale mifchief, whether internal or exter-
" nal, is commonly produced. *It would, perhaps, be*
" *prudent in the panegyrifts of refractory priefts to weigh the*
" *poffible confequences of a war with France.*"—" I cannot
" undoubtedly prove that thofe individual priefts who
" have arrived in England are not *confcientious* and *reli-*
" *gious* men. But it is reafonable to believe that the
" majority partake of the fpirit of their brethren. And
" to a large portion of the (foreign) popifh priefthood,
" Chriftianity is believed, on good grounds, to be as much
" *foolifhnefs* as it was to the Greeks.——Had thefe gen-
" tlemen reprefented the priefts as diftreffed *men* of am-
" biguous or unknown character, I hope they would
" have been equally fuccefsful in their application. The
" moft vicious, it will be univerfally allowed, fhould
" not be left to die of hunger. Of women and children,
" of the aged and infirm, the bare mention is a fufficient
" recommendation."

Treaty of Pilnitz.

I believe Lord Grenville, the firft of our miniftry,
publicly difclaimed participation in this famous compact,
laft March (1797). If the meafure was not viewed with
hopeful approbation or complacency, why was not this
declaration made while it could conciliate?

———————

IN the foregoing pages I have endeavoured, upon the
univerfally received principles of common prudence and
morality, to prove to the rich that their beft or only
chance of emerging from their prefent dangers, is to join
the reft of the people in attempting to procure a change
of miniftry. I had intended further to propofe an eafy
and cheap plan for fecuring internal tranquillity in cafe

M   of of fudden alarms. As far as regards the country, I have been anticipated by Mr. UVEDALE PRICE, a gentleman diftinguifhed by his writings on fubjects of tafte, and, I fuppofe, one of the alarmifts of 1793. Mr. Price, feeling that the minifter has gone on from day to day making our external and our internal fituation more infecure, and fearing left " defperate men," in the confufion which the landing of a foreign enemy would occafion, fhould be tempted to pillage, propofes to his Herefordfhire neighbours the following plan : They fhould, he fays, provide themfelves with arms ; and meet occafionally on horfeback, without arms or any fort of martial parade, in parties of twenty or thirty, juft as they would ride out on any other occafion. They may thus habituate their horfes to move together, exactly as well as if they were armed and accoutred. Both men and horfes would be accuftomed to each other, and well prepared for acting againft a mob.

The fame plan, applied to cities, with the exclufion of horfes, would afford at leaft equal fecurity with the new volunteer corps at far lefs trouble and expence. The force might be greater, becaufe many more individuals would and could walk together in an evening now and then in their common drefs, leaving their arms at home. The knowledge of their having arms would be a fufficient check upon perfons difpofed to feize an opportunity for general plunder.

The diforders occafioned by minifters being equally to be dreaded with thofe occafioned by mobs, and the damages fuftained from the former far greater, it fhould be underftood that fuch a fcheme would indirectly fecure our property and liberty againft this danger.

The

The nature of Mr. Price's excellent plan will appear from the following extracts: " Its great advantage is, that " it makes no difference whatsoever in the situation of " those who enter into it, either in their way of living or " the general disposition of their time." " It may possibly " be proposed to you to have officers appointed by govern- " ment, or to be attached to the Yeomanry Cavalry. In " this case you would, like them, be liable to be com- " manded out of the county ; and so far from consenting " to that, you ought not to be commanded in it. For, " in my decided opinion, that would destroy the whole " advantage of our union. Your place is on your own " premises, where your daily occupations are equally " useful to your country and to yourselves ; and where " you are always in readiness to defend what it is your " first duty and purpose to protect from every injury, " your own and your neighbours property. The great " point, therefore, on which your own welfare, and the " use which you may render to your country, depends, is, " that you should not be subject to any military regula- " tions in any shape or form whatsoever, but that you should " remain precisely in the same situation in which you are " at present, under the controul of the laws and the di- " rection of the civil magistrate."

Thoughts on the Defence of Property.

This, I think, will be felt as the only principle of in- terior security for a country like Great Britain. None other is consistent with common sense and oeconomy, and at the same time efficacious.

FINIS.